50 Ways
To Live Life
Consciously

Christine Agro

Haldi Press

Halid Press
PO BOX 111
Pleasant Valley, NY 12569

Copyright © 2012 Christine Agro

All rights reserved, including the right to reproduce this book or portions thereof in any form whatsoever. For information, contact Haldi Press, PO Box 111, Pleasant Valley, NY 12569

Haldi Press trade paperback edition February 2012

Cover updated: March 2018

For information about special discounts for bulk purchases please contact Haldi Press at 347-273-2962 or inquiry@haldipress.com

Manufactured in the United States of America

ISBN-10: 0982681437
ISBN-13: 978-0-9826814-3-5

DEDICATION

Life is a journey. Spiritual evolution is a spiral. Living a conscious life puts you in the driver's seat of your own magnificently spiraling journey.

To all beings whose passion, purpose and dedication are helping the collective step into conscious awareness

To Caidin – Thank you for choosing me to be your Mom. Thanks for being here. I love you.

To Chuck – my rock, my best friend, my light when it's dark. With you, life is more than I imagined.

To Mom – I love you.
To Dad – You are with me every day.

ACKNOWLEDGEMENTS

To everyone who supports me, knowingly, unknowingly, consciously, unconsciously; and to everyone who has helped me learn, heal and grow – Thank you!

A SPECIAL THANK YOU TO
Chuck Agro, Caidin Agro, Trudy and Bill Viscardo,
Gertrude Rieker,
Farida Sharan, Lauren Skye, Grace Morgan
Divya Chandra, Samantha Bachechi,
Nan Bush and Bruce Weber, Grace Coddington,
Alison Shields, Amy Sophiella, Sara Willerson,
Diane Caldwell, Maria Fregosi

Contents

A Message From Christine 1
   How Does This Book Help You? 6
   Part I: Conscious Living 9
     Life is a Journey 9
     The Mind Trap 12
         Quiet The Mind 13
         A TOOL TO QUIET YOUR MIND 13
     The Ego Trap 14
         Indications Your Ego Is Driving Your Life 15
         A TOOL TO SET ASIDE THE EGO 15
     The Validation Trap 17
         How do you know if you are seeking external validation? 19
         A TOOL FOR SELF-EMPOWERMENT 20
     The Emotional Trap 21
         A TOOL TO HELP YOU OFF THE WHEEL OF EMOTIONS ... 23
     The Neutral Zone 24
         A TOOL TO HELP YOU DEVELOP NEUTRALITY 27
         Align With Your Spirit 29
         A TOOL TO ALIGN YOURSELF WITH SPIRIT 31
     Why Am I Here? 32
         A TOOL TO HELP YOU UNCOVER YOUR LIFE LESSONS 35
     Enlightenment of the Past 37
     How To Use This Book 39
         As A 50 Week Program 39

As A Support and Guide	41
Part II: 42 Conscious Living Concepts	44
Inner Peace	47
Love	48
Compassion	49
Inner Child	50
Wisdom	51
Amusement	52
Balance	53
Water	54
Grounding	55
Intuition	56
Focus	57
Truth	58
Alignment	59
Insight	60
Freedom	61
Gentleness	62
Guidance	63
Vibration	64
Harmony	65
Create	66
Celebrate	67
Health	68
Consciousness	69
See	70

Listen	71
Speaking	72
Support	73
Joy	74
Light	75
Tools	76
Meditation	77
Music	78
Movement	79
Adventure	80
Nourish	81
Embrace	82
Explore	83
Encourage	84
Expand	85
Patience	86
Calm	87
Breathe	88
Stepping Into a Conscious Life	89
- The Choice of a Lifetime	89
Feeling Stuck?	90
TOOL TO HELP YOU BRING CONSCIOUS AWARENESS TO ALL AREAS OF YOUR LIFE	91

Christine Agro

A Message From Christine

Welcome to *50 Ways to Live Life Consciously*. I think it's nice to have some insight into who we are traveling with, so I wanted to take a minute to introduce myself and share with you a bit of my own journey to conscious living.

I live just outside of New York City with my husband Chuck, our amazingly conscious son Caidin, our dog Brew, cat Cassie and our parakeet ChaCha Blue and would love it if my mom would come live with us too.

I've been helping people live life with greater consciousness, empowerment and understanding of their own life journey for a little over 12 years.

I am a clairvoyant and a metaphysical expert as well as a Naturopath and Herbalist.

People always want to know what clairvoyance is and if I've always been clairvoyant. Here's how I explain Clairvoyance: Clairvoyance is French for "clear sightedness" and my clairvoyance manifests as the ability to see all information and experiences in their energetic form. I believe we all have this ability, but most of us are unaware of it and those that are aware of it choose not to learn how to use it, usually out of fear.

I first became aware of my ability to tap into life as energy when I was seven. It showed up as the ability to see future dramatic events like deaths and accidents before they happened. I was also clairaudient which allowed me to hear people when they weren't present. Like the time I heard my grandmother and grandfather arguing and I thought they were home, but instead they were at their country house. Today, I attribute all of this to the ability to access my higher senses . We all understand our physical senses – the ability to see, touch, hear, taste and smell; but each of these senses has a higher counterpart. The higher counterparts are the ability to see energy (Clairvoyance), hear energy (Clairaudience) , feel energy (Clairsentience). The ability to taste and smell energy are lesser used, although there have been times when information has come to me as a smell or a taste. In addition to having this strong connection to my higher senses, I also possess a strong connection to my inner wisdom – a knowingness of what is right, of who I am and that there is more to us than our physical form.

My first memorable moment of inner wisdom came to me when I was 11 or 12, at a time that was pre-Dr. Phil and pre-Oprah. The notion of self-help had just begun to surface, but certainly didn't make its way into my home or my world.

I grew up with a good deal of teasing – mostly about my physical body and physical appearance. My older brother was fond of telling me that I was stupid, fat and ugly. One day, I had the overwhelming awareness that if I didn't love myself, no one else would really be able to love me either. So I came up with an exercise that helped me to learn to love myself.

Every morning, before school, I sat in front of my beautiful floor length standing mirror, looked into my own eyes and told myself 'I love you.' It was one of the most uncomfortable things I've ever done, but little by little I developed the ability to say 'I love you' and really embrace my self-love.

Around the same time, I also created this prayer– 'May God bless me, keep me safe and free from harm and fill me with your love that I may always give it to others.' The prayer came from my inner awareness that I needed to be whole to live completely and as a child, these were the words that I felt would help me accomplish this wholeness of being.

As I grew up, I went through various trials and tribulations, but my inner guidance always led me out the other side. Looking back, it is amazing to see that at age 11, or 15 or 19 or 23, I was able to self-monitor my own behaviors and make conscious choices to live differently. I had the awareness that my actions were not in alignment with who I really was and I had the ability and the fortitude to make changes, whether that meant removing people from my life or eliminating habits and addictions.

In 1999 at the age of 34, I found myself walking to work and the thought 'How did I get here?' drifted through my mind. Now, I knew how I got to that place on the sidewalk, I hadn't totally lost my mind; but it was a moment of clarity that whispered that deeper question 'How did I get to this place in my life, doing what I do, being who I am?' At the time I was a professional fundraiser and I had both a BFA and an MBA. I was a business woman, with an important role in an important organization. But the more I thought about this question of 'How did I get here?' the less I liked it. I didn't like this feeling that I had just floated along unconsciously to this place, not a bad place mind you, but floated none-the-less and this was my wake-up call.

I had, for a longtime, been exploring psychic information and dabbling in natural healing – taking a course here and there, reading books and promising myself I would learn how to access and use my abilities. But it was this one moment in time that changed everything. I actively began to explore programs that would help me cultivate the abilities and the passion that lay inside me.

I enrolled in the Naturopathic Program, The Master Herbalist Program and the Master Iridologist Program at *The School of Natural Medicine* in Boulder and I became a student at *The Inner Connection Institute* (ICI) in Denver, a center designed to help people not only unlock their clairvoyance, but also learn how to use it in ways that benefit both the self and others. As soon as I learned how to do clairvoyant readings in class, I began doing readings for people outside of class. It was such a natural experience for me. I remember commenting to one of the teachers at ICI that I felt like I had come home.

I created great freedom by validating a part of me that had always been there, but didn't really have a place in the 'normal' world. I was learning that normal is who we truly are, it doesn't matter if my 'normal' wasn't someone else's normal too.

By 2001 I had left the world of Not-For-Profit Fundraising altogether, graduated from *The School of Natural Medicine*, lived at an ashram for a month to gain my yoga certification and stayed 3 weeks at *The Ann Wigmore Institute* in Puerto Rico to gain my Living Foods Certification. I was well immersed in setting free my inner truth.

From that moment in 1999, when that life changing question floated into my conscious awareness through to present day, I have marveled in our individual and collective journeys, using my ability to holistically see our lives as the playground of our Spiritual evolution. Through this ability to see the deeper meanings and core lessons – what are we working on and how have we set-up our lives to do this work? – I have gathered such exciting insight into the how, why and what-for of our lives. This insight has helped clients and students from all walks of life, in all parts of the world step into conscious living, conscious awareness and the gift of understanding their own amazing life journey.

When I look back at the timing of my life, I see that I was meant to be a bridge. I bridge the boomers to the gen-xers, I bridge the Indigo children to the Rainbow children and the Crystalline children, I bridge the old way to the new way of living on this planet. And I bridge the unconscious journey to the conscious journey.

This is an amazing journey we are on, full of magic and self-empowerment. As we step into consciousness, we begin to see that the power doesn't lie outside, it rests within, just waiting for us to wake it up.

So consider *me* your wake-up call. I'm calling to you, asking you to wake-up, cross the bridge and step into your own amazing conscious life full of things to learn, full of things to heal and full of ways to grow.

As Spirits with the wonderful fortune of having manifested physical form, we have and are so much. In our current state of awareness (which in truth is pretty unconscious) we have barely scratched the surface of who we are, what we can do and how we can live.

I share the information in this book to help you become more conscious, more aware and more empowered. Things are changing fast on our planet, and Conscious Living, embracing all that we are from a deeper level of awareness, will be our saving grace. The chaos and crumbling structures are not things to fear, but serve as their own wake-up call. They are akin to having the carpet pulled out from under us. We have been sleeping for so long and not paying attention to the gentle messages telling us that we need to live differently, that we are now getting the very loud, very incapable-of-being-ignored messages that we must change.

How Does This Book Help You?

This book offers you 8 tools and 42 concepts, each of which will help you in creating a conscious connection between your Spirit and your body. Each concept will support you as you travel your unique path of learning about and earning the right to harness the unlimited power that is waiting within for you to embrace.

To live life consciously it requires conscious choice. It requires that you openly accept the process of becoming a fully conscious being. At this level of growth and awareness, we are long past the days of asking for our next step or having guidance fall into our laps. At this level, you must initiate the journey, you must consciously take the steps to create change in your life and you must consciously choose to walk forward each and every day.

During this process you may experience challenges. Challenges are your Spirit's way of asking 'are you sure you want to do this?' Challenges can come in any shape or form, but you will know them because you will find yourself questioning whether growing is worth it or possibly whether you are wasting your time. Each step of the way we are given the opportunity to stop our growth and stay right where we are, just as we are given the opportunity to continue moving forward. Conscious living is ultimately about choice – what do you choose?

50 Ways to Live Life Consciously gives you guidance in your process of seeing yourself as something more than just your physical body. To create change in your life, it requires a decided choice to do things differently, to live differently, to see differently, to do life differently.

If you say 'Yes" to change, I can't promise you that change will be easy, but I can tell you that living life consciously IS what life is all about.

Feel free to stop by TheConsciousLivingGuide.com where you can become a member and join a community of like-minded individuals all moving toward living life consciously. You'll find different levels of participating, from the BASIC membership to add-on courses that will help you transform your life.

Remember LIFE is not about getting somewhere, it's about what you do, learn, heal and create along the way.

This book will give you a whole new way of looking at your journey and even if you read just one page, you will be more conscious than you were before you opened this book.

As always…

Thanks for being here!

Christine Agro

Part I: Conscious Living

Life is a Journey

Life is a journey; a journey that can be full of grace and ease, but only if we live life with conscious awareness. To live with conscious awareness means that we understand how our life works, why we are here, and how our life has been put together. Nothing in our lives occurs by accident or by mistake. Everything that happens leads us to fulfilling the purpose of our life. What is a mistake is believing that our life purpose is something outside of ourselves, something that we will do, or become. Our life's purpose is simply to evolve as Spiritual beings; to learn, to heal and to grow. It is through the process of 'life' that we get to fulfill this purpose most efficiently and most completely. All of the trials and tribulations are the ways in which we unconsciously learn, heal and grow. They are the opportunities set up by us as Spirit – our higher-self -to learn the lessons that will help us evolve in consciousness and being. The struggles we experience happen because in our unconsciousness we need something to push and pull against. Something that will create the tension in our life that propels us to seek answers, to make decisions and hopefully experience our learning, healing and growth.

Two common experiences connected to unconscious growth are 1) to have the same experience come up over and over again and 2) to experience both ends of the spectrum for a given situation.

So in the first – let's take a job as an example (although it could just as easily be a relationship) – Ellie is miserable in her job. She feels undervalued, unrecognized and she finds her job to be a constant source of dissatisfaction in her life. So she looks for a new job, maybe even in a different field. She gets a new job and it's great for maybe 3 months or 6 months and then she finds herself having the same experiences that she was having at her old job.

What needs to change isn't the job or where she works, or the people she works with, what her Spirit is asking Ellie to address is the lessons she wants to learn – in this case – that her validation must come from within, not from what others think about her, or the recognition she receives or the position she holds.

In the second example –let's look at a relationship – Ellie's in a relationship where she cares deeply for Michael and she does everything for him. There is nothing that she won't do, nothing that she won't give up, in fact, she gives up much of who she is to be in this relationship. Eventually, Ellie reaches a point where she starts to feel angry and recognizes that the relationship is all give and no take and she ends the relationship. Ellie feels invigorated and experiences a great sense of personal power as she rediscovers herself. Her next relationship she finds herself with the shoe on the other foot. Ellie meets a wonderful man, Richard, and he cares about her deeply and will do anything for her, and he gives and gives and gives. Ellie at first feels like she is living in a fairytale, until one day she realizes she's lost herself again. For all of Richard's generosity, love and kindness, she can't take it anymore. She wants to do things for herself, find her own way, fix her own problems. So Ellie breaks it off and is again invigorated and experiences a great sense of personal power as she rediscovers herself. Ellie can go back and forth like this forever, experience both ends of the spectrum in her relationships and nothing will change unless she realizes that the lesson she is trying to learn is similar to the first example –validation doesn't come by giving ourselves away nor does it come by someone else seeing us. Validation comes from within – the ability to know that we are whole and complete in and of ourselves. But without conscious awareness, Ellie can continue to try on different jobs and different partnerships, hoping to find the 'right' ones, but at the end of the day, it is her own healing and growth that should be the focal point. Once Ellie begins to live life consciously and begins to understand the journey of her life, she can learn to validate herself and in turn both her work and personal relationships will be dramatically different.

When we live unconsciously our life drives us. We find ourselves in places and experiencing things without knowing how or why we got to where we are. Instead of consciously choosing the how , the why and in what we experience life, it is our life that pulls *us* along. With conscious living we recognize that our life experiences hold the keys to what our life lessons are all about. With that we can make conscious choices about how our own life unfolds and each choice leads us further down our path of Spiritual evolution.

Our Spiritual evolution is why we are here in the first place: to learn, heal and grow as Spiritual beings. We have been taught that we are merely our physical bodies, that we are merely human beings and that our lives are all about what we do. But there is so much more to who we are and who we can be and so much more to living our lives.

The Mind Trap

We have been taught through science, through educational institutions, through society and through culture that we are nothing more than our physical form. We are taught that what can be proved, quantified or studied in some concrete way is what matters and what is relevant. Things we can't see, or prove, or quantify are pushed aside, unless they can ultimately be proven. This is driven by the mental body. For centuries, even eons our minds have been a driving factor. What we know, what we see, how we interpret what we experience – our mind has been calling the shots. With this control we are locked into a life of analytics, assessment and questioning that keeps us running on a hamster wheel – ultimately going nowhere.

When the mind is controlling our journey it tries to figure out what the next step is, or how we are going to get ourselves into a different experience. The problem with the mind leading is that it is actually limited in what it can comprehend. It is limited by what we have learned, and there are so many more possibilities beyond that.

It is the mind that creates anxiety, fear, suspicion, doubt and self-sabotage. It is the mind that creates a loop in which a situation is gone over and over, seeking a solution or a different outcome, but neither can occur through thought. Change will only occur by having a conscious awareness of the life lesson at hand and your solution will come through insight inspired by your higher-self. That will create real growth and change and allow you to move forward.

Quiet The Mind

Quieting the mind doesn't mean not using it, it just means training your mind to get off the hamster wheel so that you can actually receive the messages your spirit tries to send you. As long as you let your mind run the show, you will continue to travel unconsciously through your life.

This simple tool can help you quiet your mind, but be prepared to practice, practice, practice before your mind gives up its starring role in your life.

A TOOL TO QUIET YOUR MIND
Creating Quiet With Your Breath

- Sit in a chair.
- Close your eyes.
- Have your feet flat on the floor.
- Take a deep breath in and let it out.
- Bring your attention to the space right behind your eyes (eyes are still closed)
- Now focus your breath into this space continuing to take long, deep, slow breaths.
- Let your only focus be on your breath, in and out of this space behind your eyes.

As you practice this quieting exercise begin to listen for answers and be open to insight. As you learn to quiet your mind, answers and insight may come during this exercise, or they may show up while in the shower, as you drift off to sleep or even through your dreams. The more you can offer quieting support to your mind, the more you will be able to hear the messages sent by your higher-self.

The Ego Trap

Our egos have also played into our unconscious existence. Believing that our self-worth is something that we find through achievement, accomplishment or recognition, our ego leads us to push, strive and reach for validation in ways that may not be in harmony with the Spiritual plan of our higher-self -the plan of our own lives.

The plan of our life is connected to what you came here to work on not who you are supposed to be, or what you are supposed to do with your life – these things rather are the ego directing and guiding you to find validation in sources outside of your own inner knowing.

The ability to validate yourself, to know from within that you are worthy and important simply in the fact that you are here, creates not only a connection to your own consciousness but a freedom that is priceless.

It is important to remember that the ego has two ends of the spectrum with a range of activity in between. It is the bragging, forceful aspect just as much as it can be the shy and withdrawn. We tend to miss the fact that our need to not be seen, to not stand-out because of fear that we won't measure up, is equally an ego dynamic. Because of this, some of the signs your ego is running your life might actually surprise you as we tend to associate the ego with bragging and the 'me, myself and I' syndrome.

Indications Your Ego Is Driving Your Life
- The use of me, myself and I
- A need to be recognized
- A need to be seen as unique or special
- The use of force of will to make things happen
- Your life is full of effort and work
- Bragging
- Validating the self through external experience
- Bullying (bullying can be verbal, emotional, physical or energetic – energetic bullying is the process of pushing someone around through the use of your energy – being energetically bigger than someone.)
- Shyness
- Timidity
- Fear
- Retreat
- Hermit-like tendencies

A TOOL TO SET ASIDE THE EGO
Light-Up Your Soul

Our soul is the energetic core of our being. Where our Spirit is the guide and director, our soul holds the light of who we are intrinsically. Unfortunately for many of us, our life experiences have covered, hidden and/or dimmed the light of our soul, leaving the ego working overtime in an effort to find some way to heal or activate our inner light.

Our soul sits within us, midway behind our 3rd and 4th chakras. Chakras are energy centers within the body. Each chakra has it's own unique vibration and is associated with different aspects of our total being. Meaning 'wheel' in Sanskrit, chakras appear to the clairvoyant eye as balls of energy within the body. The 3rd chakra is located at the solar plexus and unbalanced it represents the energies of will, force and control. When balanced it represents the energies of true personal power or the power of our Spirit. The 4th chakra is located where our heart is and this chakra holds the energies of self-worth, love and compassion. Unbalanced it can manifest as greed, speed, lack and limit. Balanced we have abundance and flexibility in our lives.

It is important to understand the energies of these two chakras as when unbalanced they both fuel the need of the ego to direct our life.

If the energies of the 3rd and 4th chakras are burning clear and balanced, the 3rd fuels the 4th allowing us to live a life of passion and purpose. If they are cluttered and unbalanced we experience the push-pull of our ego trying to control our life.

Rather than focusing on individually healing the 3rd and 4th chakras, we can focus on uncovering and activating our own soul. By infusing our own soul with light, the soul is acknowledged and activated and it burns brighter and brighter, naturally clearing and balancing the energies of both the 3rd and 4th chakras.

Light-Up And Activate Your Soul

- Sit in a chair with your feet flat on the floor.
- Close your eyes.
- Take a nice deep breath in and let it out.
- Take your finger and find the spot that is midway between your solar plexus (where the ribcage splits) and your physical heart (center of your chest right between your breasts or pecs) There isn't a big space between these two points.
- Once you have the spot, draw an imaginary line from this back toward your spine and settle your attention there.
- Begin to send light to this area, the seat of your soul.
- Feel it getting warmer.
- See it getting brighter and brighter.
- Let the light and warmth from the soul radiate through the solar plexus and heart and let it continue to expand through your entire body as well as out from your body.
- Practice this tool daily until your soul is fully charged and activated.

The Validation Trap

The ego as driver is strongly connected to where your validation, commonly known as your sense of self, comes from. Any form of external validation requires that you give your own power away in order to receive recognition or self-worth from an external source. Learning to self-validate, to know that you are good, worthy, important, relevant, needed, and loved regardless of what you do in the world, who is in your life or who approves of you, can set you free.

Sometimes the concept of validation can elude us, especially if it is a key life lesson. Validation in this sense means to make valid or confirm validity of our own existence. A major part of our life's journey is to learn that we are worthy, in and of our own self, and that we are in need of no one to tell us that we are o.k., that we are enough, or that we matter. Without this self-knowledge we live with an emptiness and we look outside ourselves to fill it. The life lesson is to learn that our fulfillment, that sense of being full, must come from within. To learn that we are good, we are worthy, we matter from within, will change your life. Your actions will no longer be predicated on who noticed, who applauded, who valued your contribution; your actions will emanate from a place of self-awareness.

When I was in the business world, I knew my own worth. I was very clear of what I contributed to an organization, the value I added by my presence and I also knew that no matter what job I held, that I was capable and added something relevant and important. I didn't need someone to approve, applaud or tell me I was doing a good job. What this gave me was freedom. Freedom from needing to hear 'good job' from my boss, freedom from needing to compete with co-workers and the freedom to know my own worth. On a number of occasions, because my validation came from within and I knew my own worth, I was able to negotiate raises based on factual information – comparisons to salaries of others in the same field, and a demonstration of my contributions. The raises were warranted. They did not come from a place of feeling the need to receive more in order to be validated.

We also carry this same emptiness in our relationships. Jealousy and feeling undervalued in relationships both stem from looking for fulfillment from the outside: Am I enough? Do you love me? What will I be if you are not in my life? Please acknowledge what I do and what I contribute.

When we learn to self-validate, we fill ourselves with the knowingness that we are enough, we are lovable and we matter. When we can self-validate, we no longer give our power away, which is what happens when we seek validation from others. In order to receive the energy that fills us and makes us whole, we have to give something in return and in this case we give away our own power to fill from within.

Self-validation continues to be a gift in my life as I do not need validation from clients, my family or my friends. I know what I bring to the world. I know that I matter and I know that my ability to fill myself with my own self-worth is what empowers me.

How do you know if you are seeking external validation?

- You ask people to confirm your statements.
- You look to others to approve of your choices

- You are uncertain of your own worth unless someone else confirms it
- You do not feel complete unless you are loved
- You do not feel complete unless you are acknowledged

We seek external validation because within we are empty. We are empty because we have not learned to self-validate. This is why learning to self-validate is a key life lesson for many of us. When we no longer need to look outside ourselves for the message that we are ok, that we are enough, and that we matter, we step into consciousness and our own self-empowerment.

A TOOL FOR SELF-EMPOWERMENT
Learning To Self-Validate

- Sit in a chair.
- Place your feet flat on the floor.
- Close your eyes.
- Imagine a big horseshoe magnet out in front of you and use it to call all your power back to you into an energetic bubble. We give our power away when we accept validation from outside sources.
- Move that energetic bubble above your head, pop it and fill yourself with your own power.
- Next, create another bubble above your head.
- Fill this bubble with self-validation. You can intend it, pretend it, imagine it or see it – it all works. There is no right or wrong way for self-validation to look – it may be a color, or an image, or a word or simply the sense of self-validation.
- Once the bubble is good and full, pop it and fill yourself in with your own validation.

Do this exercise over and over again. The more you fill in with you, the less you will need others to fill you in.

The Emotional Trap

Are you familiar with that saying 'Don't let your emotions get the best of you?' Somewhere, we know that letting our emotions control us is counterproductive. When our emotions run the show we get hooked by experiences and encounters that completely take us off track and out of our power. The Emotional Trap is often coupled with The Validation Trap, because it is in our need to be seen, appreciated or approved of by others that we find ourselves emotionally charged – whether we get angry, sad, depressed or frustrated.

Being ruled by emotions can be another *hamster wheel* dynamic. We can't move forward as long as we are running on the wheel of our emotions.

Let's look at Ellie again. In Ellie's day-to-day life she is a competent, successful 45 year old business woman who balances her own family and her career. Although her life is stressful and things could be better, she is a grown-up in a grown-up world. That is, until she walks through the door of her parents' home. The minute she takes that step over the threshold she is hooked by the comments her mom makes. They are insinuating, snide and infuriating and Ellie is hooked emotionally, back on the wheel of emotions and thrown right back to identifying with herself as a fourteen year-old girl.

The power, the awareness and the information that we had when we were fourteen or eight or five is but a fraction of what we have today, yet many of us react and respond in many situations at an age far less than what we actually are. Ellie is a grown woman who has accomplishments and a life to celebrate, but in her need to be validated (seen, acknowledged, loved) by her mother she gives all of that away, all of her power away, in the hopes that her mother will see her. In that action, she reverts back and reacts and responds from the information, awareness and level of personal power that she had as a teenage girl.

A similar dynamic can occur in situations where we are uncomfortable, like in public speaking for example. I personally used to have a very hard time speaking in public, to the point of hyper-ventilating – it wasn't a pretty sight. Until one day, several years into the process of exploring my own conscious growth and healing, I found myself preparing to speak to a group of 200 people about a new way to work with and see animals from an energetic and spiritual perspective. I was so anxious and nervous. My heart was pounding, and my mouth was dry. I was certain hyper-ventilation was just around the corner. Then, in a moment of clarity I realized, I was showing up as a fifteen-year-old. What did I know as a fifteen-year-old? What information, self-knowledge, and experiences did I have at that age? No wonder it was so hard to get up and speak in front of people. I was not standing in my full power or in my full truth. As soon as I made the shift, the change was almost miraculous.

I no longer felt anxious or nervous and ever since I have been able to share my own information from a fully empowered, fully conscious place.

A TOOL TO HELP YOU OFF THE WHEEL OF EMOTIONS
How Old Am I?

All you need to do with this tool is stop and ask yourself, "How old am I right now?" and then listen for the answer. The answer might arrive as a knowingness, or you may hear it or you may see an image of yourself that indicates a specific time in your life.

You can also sit in a quiet meditative space and look at any relationship or situation to explore the same questions.

- Sit in a chair with your feet flat on the floor
- Close your eyes
- Take a nice deep breath in and let it out
- Imagine out in front of you is a timeline that runs from birth to your current age.
- Now think about the relationship or the situation you'd like to explore and ask "How old am I?"
- On the time-line a light will turn on to show you how old you are in this situation.

Here are just a few examples of what you can look at: How old am I when I'm talking to my mom? How old am I when I'm talking to my boss? How old am I when I have to speak what is true for me?

There is no limit to how you can use this tool or to the information you can gather about how you show up in the world. Once you have this awareness, you can now begin the process of showing up as the 'you' of today rather than the 'you' of the past.

How we respond emotionally, whether we continue to be hooked by our emotions and our need to be validated affects greatly our ability to live life consciously and in present time.

The Emotional Trap keeps you locked into reactions and experiences from the past and will keep you striving to heal the wounds from that place-in-time.

Our wounds can include things like being dismissed or diminished by comments and actions and these things may not have been intentional. Our wounding can come from the best efforts of those closest to us to guide and teach us – but the wounding happens none-the-less. I say this because it does us no good to blame others for the healing we seek. Look at what you were trying to learn in these situations and then start to heal through this insight.

Learning to self-validated is one of the greatest gifts you can give yourself and will help release you from the emotional trap.

The Neutral Zone

Another great tool to explore in releasing the hold emotions have on our lives is neutrality. Neutrality is the ability to *not* get hooked by comments or situations. Getting hooked is a game that keeps our energy focused on things that don't benefit us. It's a game that keeps us from living life consciously and fully.

Developing neutrality gives you the ability to be in any environment or any situation and know that within your own space you are enough. The drama and chaos that others create in their own lives is a way for them to receive external validation. Your willingness to participate means that you are giving your power away to others so that they can feel validated. Now, you may think 'why would someone create chaos to be validated?' Unfortunately we learn very early in life that negative behavior gives us attention, negative as it may be, it is still a way to be seen and a way of receiving external validation.

Let's look at another example with Ellie. Ellie stops by her mom's to pick up some mail that got delivered. She's been working all day, it's been a hectic day and she's tired. She walks through the door and her mom says 'You know honey it wouldn't hurt if you wore a little make-up, you're looking really old.' Ellie's reaction is to feel hurt and demeaned and she says nothing. But she's thinking "geez Mom, why can't you just give me a hug and say 'it looks like you had a hard day'" Ellie lets her mother have power over how she feels. Ellie knows herself that she's had a hard day. Does she need her mom to validate her for it, or make it better for her? If she does, she's on both the emotional wheel and the validation wheel.

If Ellie can have neutrality and see this not as a personal slight, but simply as the way in which her mother communicates; a way that is based in the experiences and wounding of her mother's own life; then Ellie can have neutrality. Her mother can think or say whatever she wants, but it only effects Ellie if she lets it *and* if she needs her mother to validate her.

Learning this lesson is so empowering, but it is one of the most difficult lessons to learn, which is why it often shows up in a parent/child relationship. At the Spirit level this parent holds the space for you to learn to self-validate and through their actions, continually pushes you to learn this lesson.

If you have a wonderful parent relationships look for where this dynamic might exist in other important relationships: a sister, brother, grandparent, partner, spouse.

For some people, especially those who have been ruled by their emotions, developing neutrality is challenging and the whole concept may seem foreign. When a concept is connected to a major life lesson, the meaning of the concept can be hard to grasp. So in this case, learning to be neutral, or to release your emotional reaction may be so foreign to you, that the whole concept of neutrality is just out of reach.

I find that looking at the definition of a word can help bring clarity to how the concept can support us. I define neutrality as: the ability to allow others to have their opinions, beliefs and practices while knowing that these have nothing to do with who you truly are. It is a state of non-engagement, no opinion and no reaction to those things that have nothing to do with us.

When we develop neutrality, it gives us a clear perspective. We are able to look at situations as an observer and recognize that it is our choice to engage or not engage, rather than unconsciously getting lost as a participant in someone else's drama or opinion.

A TOOL TO HELP YOU DEVELOP NEUTRALITY
Developing Neutrality

This exercise can help you to develop neutrality. This is one of those exercises that requires regular practice in order to create change. The more you play with this tool, the greater your neutrality will become. You may also notice that through this process, you require far less external validation.

To begin with:

- Sit in a chair with your feet flat on the floor.
- Close your eyes and take a nice deep breath in and out.
- Place your finger in the center of your forehead just above the bridge of your nose (at the place of your third eye or 6th chakra).
- Draw all of your attention and energy right behind your finger.
- As you sit like this, your focus is on keeping your attention and energy inside your own head, right behind this finger.
- It may help to envision a spot of light at this point – so that when you are sitting and focusing you are focusing on that single spot of light.
- Remember to keep pulling your attention and energy into this spot.

Begin with this to start. Practice this tool daily. As the process of keeping your attention and energy within increases, take your practice to this **next step:**

- With your eyes open, practice bringing your attention and energy into this same place – center of your head, just above the bridge of your nose. It may help at first to return to placing your finger at this spot.

This exercise can be an interesting experience as for many, our actual vision can shift when we pull ourselves into neutrality while our eyes are open. How you see can change when you see through your own neutrality.

After you gain a level of comfort being neutral with your eyes open, it's time to take your practice out into the world.

Developing neutrality is a flow and ebb process. We get it, we don't get it, we get it, we don't get it. The times when you 'get it' give you an opportunity to see what your life can be like when you have neutrality. The times when you don't 'get it' give you a reminder of 1) where you aren't neutral and have greater work to do and 2) what it is like when you are hooked by our emotions and a need for external validation.

Taking Your Neutrality Practice Out into the World

A great way to start is to give yourself an assignment. If you are hooked or challenged by your mother or your boss or maybe the evening news – give yourself the play assignment to explore neutrality in this situation. Go into the situation knowing that you want to be neutral, pull your attention and energy into that space in the center of your head and see what happens.

Remember – it's play, it's all an exploration of your own learning, growing and healing and each opportunity you have to explore your neutrality is another step closer to getting off the wheel of emotions.

Align With Your Spirit

If neither your ego, your mind nor your emotions run the show, then who does? Your Spirit, more commonly referred to as your higher-self. I like to avoid the term 'higher-self' though because it implies that our Spirit is above us or not connected. In truth, the more consciously we live our lives and the more our mind and ego make room for Spirit to guide, our Spirit is a very present and very much an active part of our day-to-day living. In fact, it is our life. Until now though, your Spirit has been hanging out, waiting for you to recognize this, just waiting for this moment of conscious awakening.

Several years ago I began exploring what it meant for Spirit to lead. I had many questions: How does this work? How do I allow Spirit to lead? What does it look like? I was guided to play with the notion of 'aligning with my Spirit', to put all of the aspects of my being in alignment with my Spirit, so that Spirit was at the front, or in the lead, or the top of line. I played with many ways of 'seeing' this and creating alignment, interestingly they all work and this process of aligning has become an integral component of living life consciously. As we create a natural alignment between the Spirit, the ego, the mind and the emotions we reprogram our inherited, unconscious approach to living life. Through alignment, we encourage the mind, the ego and the emotions to step into their supporting roles rather than controlling roles. It is our Spirit that has the roadmap to our life. You created yours before you were born and it includes exactly what you wanted to learn, heal and evolve this lifetime. When we learn to align with our Spirit, that's when conscious living begins as it is through this alignment that you can be guided along your true life's journey.

This exercise will also require practice to create a change within. After years, and maybe even lifetimes of your mind, ego and emotions running the show, your being is conditioned to believe that without their guidance and leadership, you can't survive. Now that we have the ability to live consciously, leaving these in charge will only keep you unconscious and out of alignment with all that your Spirit wants for you and can offer you. If you practice this tool every day for a focused 30 minutes over a two week period, and include an on-going awareness of your alignment throughout the day, you will find that your consciousness will begin to open and a grace and easy will enter your life.

A TOOL TO ALIGN YOURSELF WITH SPIRIT
Learning To Align

- Sit in a chair.
- Close your eyes.
- Take a deep breath in and let it out.
- Imagine a straight line running through your body from the base of your tailbone up through the top of your head
- Allow and/or encourage the energy in your solar plexus (spot where the rib cage splits) to snap to the line running through your body.
- Allow and/or encourage the mind and the energy in your brain to also snap to this center line.
- Imagine the ego and mind sitting nicely on that line – ego at the solar plexus and mind in the head.
- At the top of the head imagine your Spirit or higher-self sitting also on that line.
- The image is your Spirit at the top of the line, then the brain and then the ego.
- Sit and notice what it is like to allow Spirit to lead you.

Combine this exercise with the exercises to Quiet The Mind, Self-Validate and Set The Ego Aside. Remember the process of change takes about two-weeks of constant, conscious focus and attention in order to shift old ways of operating. Keep a journal (or use the Conscious Living Playbook) to help you monitor your growth experiences. Write down what you notice, what you experience, what your day-to-day life is like when you practice these exercises.

Why Am I Here?

Ok, so now you are aligned with your Spirit and your mind, ego and emotions are getting comfortable with their new roles as supporting members of this exciting journey. "Why Am I Here?" is possibly the oldest existential question., but that's because we ask it from our mind – trying to understand and comprehend life from the limits of what we know; or because we ask it from our ego – trying to manufacture purpose and self-value by 'doing'.

At one point I was going to write an entire book on this question, but the answer is so simple that all it really requires is a single sentence. We are here to evolve our own spiritual consciousness and to play our part in the evolution of the collective consciousness of all humanity. The collective consciousness is the sum total of all energies, it is the one, it is the source of all things. Each of us is a part of this whole and our individual evolution supports the evolution of the whole.

'Why we are here' is that simple – at least in concept, but to do – well, that's a whole other ballgame, one that is full of spiritual agreements, lessons and lifetimes of playing the good, the bad and the downright ugly. In order to grow in our own conscious awareness we must play different roles; being victim and victimizer, being rich and poor, being selfless and selfish; all so that as Spirit we can understand the full spectrum of being human. This process of evolving our individual and collective consciousness has been going on since the dawn-of-time with each of our Spirits inhabiting different forms of life in order to evolve both Spiritually and physically. For most however this process has been done unconsciously, without an awareness of why we are here or what we are doing and with the mind and ego making up reasons and needs and explanations. In part this unconsciousness has kept us evolving due to the constant search for 'something more' and in looking for an answer to 'what is missing?' – like a built in code that pushes us to continue to create, explore, discover, learn and grow.

Uncovering Your Life Lessons

So here you are today, in this lifetime, stepping into your growing consciousness, starting to understand the big picture of life itself. How do you know what your life lessons are? What is it in this lifetime that will help move your own consciousness forward and support the growth of the collective? Most of us today are working on learning to self-validate so definitely spend some time reflecting on that section.

After that, there are a handful of lessons that form the base of what we are working on this lifetime. How you have built your lessons upon that base will be as unique as our fingerprints, but the base lessons are status quo.

- Stand in your truth – which includes knowing your truth, speaking your truth and living your truth
- Self-validation – the ability to be full with your own energy, your information, your own truth and to know and believe in your own worth

- Stand in your power – the ability to draw upon your inner knowingness as a source of strength and certainty.

How do you know then what exactly you are working on this lifetime? It can take some detective work to uncover and get to the root of your life lessons, but gaining the conscious awareness of what you are working on can change everything. As you step into awareness of your own life lessons, you will no longer need the drama and the outside forces to help you learn. Right now, we use the drama in our relationships to help us in taking steps forward.

Consider the first example from the beginning of the book where Ellie is seeking external validation through her job. The dynamics that she experiences, the unhappiness, the dissatisfaction, the need to change jobs – all of this is 'drama' that challenges her to learn the lesson that self-worth comes from within not from what we do or how people see us. If Ellie can see that this is what she is working on, she will then know that wherever she goes, whatever she does, she will be working on this lesson. It is not about the job, it is a life lesson for her. As Ellie learns to self-validate, the need to have these situations to help her learn this life lesson go away. Life flows.

A TOOL TO HELP YOU UNCOVER YOUR LIFE LESSONS

- Step 1: focus on one aspect of your life at a time and repeat this exercise for each aspect listed:
    - intimate relationships (look at each one separately),
    - work relationships(look at key colleagues and supervisors separately),
    - work – what you do for a living,
    - personal life – key friendships(look at each one individually),
    - relationship with mother,
    - relationship with father,
    - relationship with sister,
    - relationship with brother
- Step 2: think about this aspect and write down what works or worked. What do you like? What do you enjoy?
- Step 3: think about this aspect and write down what doesn't work. What drives you crazy? What makes you want to run away? How do you feel in this relationship or situation?
- Step 4:Take one statement from Step 3 and start to break this down until you get to a single thought or concept that describes what you are trying to learn in this relationship or situation.

- Step 5: Write down what your lesson is.

Let's use an example:

We join Ellie using this tool to explore her relationship with her brother:

- Step 1: Ellie is looking at her relationship with her brother.
- Step 2: What works: nothing, well, we used to be close but we aren't now.
- Step 3: What doesn't work: He's a bully. He's not happy unless I agree with him. He uses intimidation to get his way.
- Step 4: He's not happy unless I agree with him. I have to think the same thing he does. His information needs to be mine, but it's not. I have my own thoughts and my own beliefs.
- Step 5: My lesson with my brother is: To stand in my own truth.

Use a journal or your Conscious Living Playbook and begin to explore your key relationships. The more you understand what you want to learn this life time, the more you can let go of the unconscious ways in which you have been learning.

Enlightenment of the Past

In the past, living life with conscious awareness has been called 'enlightenment'. The difference is that in the past, when we reached a state of enlightenment it oftentimes signaled the end of our physical life – it meant transcending to a higher plane or higher level of existent which was out of our physical body. It meant a return to Spirit. The reason for this is because as spirit in human bodies, we weren't ready to manage the amazing power that comes when spirit and body are connected consciously.

When Spirit and body are connected; when we align ourselves with Spirit and allow our spirit to guide; when our mind and our ego do not have the need to control our actions; the power of our Spirit is infinite, it knows no limits or boundaries. When our Spirit is fully connected with our physical body we are then able to channel the power of our Spirit through our body, accessing all that Spirit is.

Ascended masters have demonstrated what is possible when we live as Spirit and our body is the vehicle, not the driver of our life. Ascended masters such a Jesus, Buddha, Sunat Kumara, Confucious, Mary and Kwan Yin all lived as conscious Spirit in hopes of teaching us what is possible when we live as fully connected beings.

Stepping into conscious awareness and allowing your Spirit to be at the helm of your life does require stripping away and energetically, emotionally and mentally healing that which keeps you from living fully connected. It isn't necessarily an easy journey, but there are understandable reasons that living as a fully connected being who can tap into your full Spiritual power isn't just given out like sticks of chewing gum.

Think about the Ascended Masters and the powers they displayed in their lifetimes: Instant manifestation, transmutation, the ability to heal the self and others, the ability to move things, the ability to communicate through thought, the ability to defy space and time and the list goes on. These are abilities that come with the power of living as Spirit in a physical body; all the attributes of Spirit made manifest through the physical form. But these are powers that require conscious awareness, for without conscious awareness, without the knowing and choice to live with this power, the power can be abused or manifest in unintended ways.

Think about how often you have thoughts that you don't really intend – what if you currently had the ability to instantly manifest or defy time and space? What would you be manifesting in your life and where would you be unintentionally finding yourself?

To embrace the pure power of living as Spirit with a physical body requires conscious living. It also requires consciously embracing the notion that you are Spirit with a physical body, you are more than just your physical form. Choosing to live life consciously is traveling the path of learning, healing and growing that will prepare you to harness the power that comes along with this complete and total experience of living as a fully empowered being.

We are always free to stay unconscious and our journeys are as unique as we are. One person may pick up this book and immerse themselves in the process of living life consciously, another may dabble and still another may stop and start only to stop again. Each experience is valid, each experience is part of a unique journey.

How To Use This Book

There is no right or wrong way to approach growth as each step you take will lead you to another. I am a firm believer that whatever road we travel, whatever choices we make, spiritually there are no 'wrong' choices. Every choice offers us something to learn about our path. Of course some choices result in positive experiences and some result in negative experiences. I believe that these negative experiences are connected to decisions made by the mind and the ego. The positive experiences are a manifestation of the grace and flow that happens when Spirit guides us. When we live life consciously, when we understand what we are working on and when we start to see how we have unconsciously setup our lives to help us learn, we are empowered with the opportunity to create life as we choose. Once we live with conscious awareness, the negative experiences disappear because we no longer need them as fuel for our own growth.

So there is no right or wrong way to use this book. I can offer you a few options, but feel free to create your own way of using it.

As A 50 Week Program

You can use this book as a 50 week program by beginning with exploring each of the 7 tools at the beginning of the book– one a week; and then moving on to reading one concept a week and applying it to your life actively and consciously for an entire week.

Finish the 50 weeks with the final tool which you will find at the end of the book.

As you undergo this process, consider using a journal or the Conscious Living Playbook to record your experience. Notice if *or* how your life changes – consider these questions:

- Does your life flow more easily?
- Do you have more time?
- Do you feel more supported?
- Do you feel more in charge of your own life?
- Are things happening that you'd only dreamed of?
- Do things come more easily?
- Are you happier?
- Do you feel a greater sense of connection?
- For individual tools and concepts: what happens when you use this tool or employ this concept?
- What happens when you don't?

These are just a few questions to help you explore your experience of using this book as a 50 week program. Some tools and concepts may create more change for you than others. Notice what your first reaction is and then be conscious of whether incorporating this information is easy or difficult. If you experience resistance to tools and concepts it is a good indication that good things are waiting to emerge from all that resistance.

As A Support and Guide

You can use this book as a support and guide in your everyday life. When you need insight, grab your book, flip to a page and see what concept you turn to. Our higher-self is always helping us gain insight and guidance when we have questions. You can use anything in this same way to gain insight – a dictionary, a magazine, the bible. It will be your challenge to figure out how the information connects to your own life experience – but support and guidance can always be found when we ask for it.

As with the 50 week program, you may want to keep track of the messages you receive. If you find yourself opening to the same page over and over, say for example the concept 'listen', you may want to ask for additional guidance and insight while focusing on the specific concept 'listen' and see what page you open to then.

Unlike tarot or any other form of divination – the information in this book is designed to give you the tools to create conscious awareness in your life. It is not meant to tell you what to do, what you need to do, nor to do the work for you. Conscious living is a choice, a choice to step into awareness and to focus on your learning, healing and growth with consciousness.

Do not give your power away to this information. Hold strong to the knowingness that you alone can change your life. This information is a mere tool designed to support you on your journey.

So with that…enjoy the journey!

Part II: 42 Conscious Living Concepts

Our unconsciousness is sneaky. We can think that we are seeing the full scope of our lives, but in fact we still have blinders on. Movies like *Vanilla Sky* with Tom Cruise and *The Matrix* with Keanu Reeves are all about our unconsciousness. These two movies use the idea of two different realities, the false reality which is induced by machinery contrasted against the true living, waking reality. That is exactly what I am talking about, only our false reality is created by our unconsciousness, rather than by some mechanistic disconnect. What contributes to our unconsciousness is a whole host of things – from history, culture, society, media, education and our families. We are programmed to limit what we can see and who we can be through repetitive messages. Some of these messages are so ingrained into human existence that the messages themselves are handed down unconsciously –meaning those who convey them don't even stop to think about the message that is being sent. For example, public schools in the United States are just becoming aware of unconscious behavior in teachers. A teacher will call on boys over girls in the areas of Math and Science classes. This is unconscious behavior that is programmed into teachers through years of personal experience and subtle messages and it is then unconsciously handed down yet again.

Western health care is another example of ingrained unconsciousness. The history of Western medicine is so programmed that very few people question the system or the information (both doctor and patient). Most people go to the doctor and expect the doctor to identify problems and then to fix these problems. This is completely unconscious behavior. As individuals we spend 24 hours a day, seven days a week, day-in and day-out with our bodies. A doctor sees us maybe once a year. If we are conscious and in tune with our physical body, we know what's working and what isn't working and we should be directing our care, not leaving it solely up to a doctor. We also have an innate ability to heal, but it requires taking responsibility for our health and wellness with things like eating right, sleeping, exercising and supporting the body naturally. Instead we unconsciously go to the doctor and accept whatever medication is prescribed without question, without considering whether there is another option that will create wellness, rather than the option of simply addressing the symptom. When we take conscious responsibility for our health and wellness we take great steps toward self-empowerment and great steps toward living life fully and consciously.

Even for those who are conscious, we can have awareness in one area of our life, but be completely unconscious in another. As an example, someone can be exploring their Spiritual awareness but be completely unconscious as to the foods they eat; or someone can be passionate about supporting the environment, but pay no attention to their own health and wellness. It is time for us to wake-up in *all* areas of our lives and to question all of the messages we are bombarded with that until now we have accepted at face value.

It is time to see ourselves as Holistic Beings – we are a total package -our physical form, our Spiritual self, our energetic bodies and the world we live in are all interconnected. To live consciously we need to see the total package, to see that everything is linked. How we see and treat ourselves is reflected in the health and wellness of the planet; and conversely how we treat the planet is reflected in how we experience our own health and wellness.

Each concept that follows offers you something to reflect upon and I encourage you to explore all the many ways that these concepts can bring conscious awareness into your life.

It isn't enough to simply 'think' about this information. True change comes when we embody it. As you read through these concepts, consider how and where you can create conscious awareness in your life by bringing the energy, meaning, and intention of these concepts more fully into your day-to-day life.

Inner Peace

Inner Peace is a calm, centered and graceful state that occurs when we are connected within. It is when we take our attention and our focus outside of our own body that inner peace disappears. With so many things going on in our lives and in the world, it can be easy to get drawn out of our inner connection. But that helps no one. Change really does come from within, so keeping your attention within will not only help you tap into a state of inner peace, but it will also, believe it or not, help the world. The changes we see inside ourselves ripple out to help change the world. Place your attention in your heart space and imagine that you are breathing in and out through your heart. This small act alone will connect you and create inner peace.

Love

You are reminded that you are infinitely loveable, but before you can receive love from another person, you must first love yourself. Love is not a one-way street. It involves learning to both give and receive love. If we are great at giving love but cannot accept love from others, we deplete ourselves. Think of love as a circle of unbroken giving and receiving. Spend some time looking deep within and acknowledge, appreciate and validate who you are. Release the critical voice that says you aren't enough, or you are flawed in some way. Replace that voice with kind, gentle and loving words about yourself. Place your focus in your heart and live from this place. Breathe in and out of your heart to expand it and open it up. With each breath in, receive love and with each breath out, give love. And remember, love is a universal energy. There is no limit to love.

Compassion

The common definition of compassion is outwardly focused. Compassion is our ability to sympathize with the experiences of others, coupled with our desire to make things better for them or alleviate their struggle, pain or distress. However, in living consciously you are being asked to, first and foremost, have compassion for yourself. We can be so hard on ourselves, especially when we wear many hats. Stop taking yourself to task for all the things you don't do or you miss, forget or overreact to. Instead, focus on the things that you actually do and that you do so well. Give yourself credit for all the many things you do, then celebrate – celebrate those things, celebrate the people for whom you do them and, most of all, celebrate yourself. You deserve it.

Inner Child

We all have a little one dancing and spinning inside of us, but how often do we find the time to stop and play? And when was the last time you looked at the world with the wonder and awe of a child? We can be so busy that we can lose touch with our inner child and so focused on accomplishing "life" that we stop experiencing the incredible world we live in. Have you ever followed a tree's experience through the seasons? It can be amazing to see it wake up after winter and sprout buds, then to watch the buds unfold and follow it through each step of its blooming. Or have you ever watched ants hard at work, finding food and carrying it back to their home? What a feat of determination. There are so many amazing things happening around us, but we gloss over most of it. It is our inner child who will be thrilled to take an extra five minutes to observe the tree or watch the ants. If nature doesn't interest you, that same sense of wonder, awe and playfulness can be ignited in many other ways: sing and dance, be silly, have ice cream for breakfast, jump in a puddle or swing on a swing. Find the joy of being alive that your inner child holds and knows so well. Do you hear the knock at your door? You're being asked to come out and play.

Wisdom

Wisdom comes from experience, both in this lifetime and throughout lifetimes. We each carry a resounding degree of knowledge and information that defines and explains our existence. It is important to remember that for each of us our wisdom is unique. Our wisdom speaks to our reality and each of us has our own unique reality. You are reminded that you can tap into your divine wisdom. There is no need to feel confused, challenged or even inadequate as you walk through the world. When we center ourselves in our heart space, the critical voice of the mind and the ego disappear. Listen to and with your heart and you will be guided by a wisdom that carries your Truth about love, life and living.

Amusement

Amusement is one of the highest energetic vibrations we can experience. It isn't merely telling jokes, although that can always help. Amusement comes from living light-heartedly. It is connected to finding joy in life, even in the crazy chaos that sometimes ensues. When we approach life with seriousness, life gets clogged with the heaviness of it all. If you can laugh about life, it will flow with grace and ease.

Balance

Balance is the holistic synergy of our outer and inner worlds. Living out of balance can take the appearance of having either too much or not enough of something. Maybe you find yourself saying "I have too much to do" or "I don't have enough time, or money or space." To find balance, you must consider your actions in both your inner and outer worlds. Our outward direction of energy is considered masculine in nature and our inward direction of energy is considered feminine. Outward is defined by the things we do and the people for whom we do them, whereas inward is defined by the things we do for ourselves. If you put everyone before you, you will not have anything left for yourself when you need it. If you cannot say "no" to people who want and need things from you, learning to set healthy boundaries will benefit you greatly. Consider making this your mantra: "Just because I can do something doesn't mean I have to." To help you gain insight into your inner and outer balance, practice the yogic asana called Tree Pose. In this pose you balance on one leg at a time. An inability to balance on your left leg indicates that your feminine energy is out of balance, as is your focus on yourself. An inability to balance on your right leg reflects an imbalance in your masculine energy as well as your outward focus. To help bring conscious awareness into your daily life, reflect on the choices you make throughout the day and consider whether they contribute to balance or imbalance in your world.

Water

Although we most identify with our solid physical structure, we are comprised of approximately 62% water. Because water has the ability to resonate with the energies of whatever it experiences, we are swayed energetically and emotionally by the experiences of everything we encounter. Imagine what would happen if you identified more strongly with that 62% of your being and provided foods, experiences, music, words, thoughts and visual stimulation that programmed your water for a healthy, happy, prosperous life. You can begin by charging the water you drink with positive thoughts. Pour a glass of water and cup your hands around the glass. Concentrate on positive thoughts. Positive thoughts have a high vibration. The vibration of these thoughts will transfer into the water, charging it with high life affirming vibration. When you drink the water, the positive vibrations will help to shift your inner world to match the high vibration in the water. Continue your transformation by consciously choosing energetic vibrations that will positively inform the 62% of your being that is water.

Grounding

When we are grounded, we have an energetic connection to the Earth that helps our body know that we are safe. The body responds to this sense of safety by experiencing calm, focus and balance. When we are grounded, it is then that our own Spirit, or higher self, can be present within us and it is then that we can live life consciously. If you are spinning your wheels or jumping from one activity or thought to another, now would be a good time to check the state of your grounding. Grounding is simple: Imagine a cord or a beam of light that connects to your tail bone and extends all the way down to the center of the earth. This grounding cord links your physical body to the earth and will help connect your Spirit and your body, in turn creating focus and balance.

Intuition

Trust your intuition! Intuition is a knowingness, a sense, a gut feeling, connected to our higher-senses of clairsentience (psychic feeling) and clairvoyance (psychic sight). Intuition offers messages from your higher-self, guiding and directing you as you live a more conscious life. The more conscious you become and the more awareness you have of your inner world, the more connected to your intuition you will become. And, as you honor, listen to and acknowledge your intuition the more powerful your intuition will become. Whatever is going on in your life right now, pay more attention to your intuition. Stop hiding it in a box under the bed. Wear it on your sleeve and see where your intuition leads you!

Focus

When we hear 'focus' we tend to think "place my attention on one specific thing with a specific intent". Yes, maybe you are being asked to focus on a project or a direction in life or maybe you are being asked to focus more on yourself. But Focus may also refer to the way in which you see things. Look at your world with greater clarity. Is your vision clear? Or do you need to wash the windows and gain a crisper view of what is going on in your world? When we choose to live life consciously, it requires that sharpen our focus and see not only what is on the surface, but what is behind the aspects of our lives. Programming and subtle messages can obscure our focus. Consider both aspects of Focus to achieve the results you desire.

Truth

Our Truth is the information that informs who we are, the choices we make and the way we see and understand the world. One of our greatest challenges can be accepting that one person's Truth can differ from another person's and two Truths can co-exist, even though seemingly at odds with each other. Our ability to speak and also hear and live our Truth rests in the energy center of our throat, or our throat/5th chakra. If your Truth has been suppressed, either through control or fear and either by your own doing or by others, you may experience issues pertaining to the throat area, such as loss of voice, sore throats, congestion in your throat or thyroid problems. In exploring conscious living, pay attention to two things: Are you living your Truth? And do you make room for the Truths of others? Because of the energetic connections to the throat, using your voice (singing and laughing, for example) can help clear old programming (information that isn't true to who we are, yet informs how we see ourselves and how we live) and allow you to resonate with the Truth of who you are

Alignment

Our higher self holds our life plan. When we are in alignment with our higher self, we experience a grace and ease to our daily life. When we are out of alignment, life just doesn't flow smoothly. It is when our ego or our mind takes control that things get bumpy. The mind and the ego work from a place of control and control is contrary to living consciously. Take some time each day to bring yourself into alignment with your higher self. Close your eyes and envision the mental, ego and emotional aspects of yourself aligning with your higher-self. Don't worry if you aren't sure what these aspects are or how to go about bringing them into alignment. Just intend the alignment and it will begin to happen. Do this exercise daily and watch your life flow.

Insight

Insight is a unique perspective that arrives through a spark of light. Well, maybe not literally, but that's what insight feels like when it hits. If you've been trying to understand a certain situation or find answers to a perplexing question, sometimes the desire to know stands in the way of that flash of light. An artist who is looking for the answer to something in his art work might take on something else while keeping the piece in question in his peripheral vision until insight offers a solution. If you aren't so sure how to go about moving a question into your preverbal peripheral vision and allowing your insight to spark, one easy way is to ask yourself a question and then open a book to a random page and see what the passage you turn to has to offer. Insight can also come through dreams, while you're in the shower (interestingly, water acts as a clarifying connector and often removes blocks to the answers we seek.) or during a chat with a friend. Give your insight room to ignite. Being too close to a situation or turning a problem over and over in your mind may be getting in the way of an insightful solution.

Freedom

What does "freedom" mean to you? When you hear that word, do you think of having no responsibilities, no time constraints or no financial worries? Maybe you think of a time that seemed simpler? In contemplating freedom, consider how has your perception of freedom stolen your freedom? Freedom is a state of being. We can certainly bring freedom into our way of life, but true freedom comes from knowing that it is you who create your reality and it is you who manifest all that you need. Once we understand this, the focus of what we need and desire moves from searching outside ourselves to creating within ourselves. If you feel constricted, open yourself up energetically with the intention to expand. Repeat this opening daily and you will begin to notice a sense of freedom and a whole new flow in your life.

Gentleness

Gentleness is a softness in your words, your voice, your touch and your approach to life. This applies to both how you treat yourself and how you interact with the world. The hardness that covers our gentleness comes from those times when we opened up to the world and experienced invalidation in return instead of acceptance. As a result, instead of approaching ourselves or the world with gentleness, we can adopt a guarded, critical, even skeptical stance. Where in your life has hardness replaced gentleness? Where can you speak more gently, touch more gently, love more gently and live more gently? Bring the notion of gentleness into your conscious awareness and focus on approaching your day with gentleness. The more you choose gentleness over hardness, the faster the covers that guard you will lift away.

Guidance

Wondering what to do next, what's your next step? Look to your spirit to guide you. Each of us has our own inner guidance. It comes from our higher-self, which holds the map of our life and what we want to learn in each lifetime. Ask for answers to or guidance about a specific question and your higher-self will respond to your request in any number of ways. Guidance can come in a dream, in the words of a song, from the pages of a book you're pushed to pick up or from a sense to be at a certain place at a specific time. Guidance can also come through messengers such as animals, the Tarot or angels. You are never alone on your journey; all you need to do is ask and be open to the guidance that comes your way.

Vibration

Laughter, love, anger and frustration are all vibrations of energy. Positive energies vibrate at a high level, while negative energies vibrate low. The higher our personal vibration, the more clearly we see, the more aligned our body and mind are with our Spirit and the more gracefully our life flows. Our health and wellness also depend on our vibration. Low vibrations invite disease in our bodies and in our lives; high vibrations promote strength and vitality. Whether we are aware of it or not, we set our vibration by the choices we make: the words we use, the thoughts we think, the music we listen to, the stories we tell, the way in which we live our lives. Fear is one of the lowest and amusement is one of the highest vibrations we can have. Pay attention to the vibrations in your life (your own, as well as those around you). To raise your vibration, simply set your intention to do so. Repeat this intention regularly throughout the day. Remember that you can choose to engage in or disengage from situations that lower your vibration. Your life is always in your hands to create as you choose.

Harmony

When we understand the Universal Law of Harmony, we realize that we can co-exist with everyone, no matter what place they are at emotionally, mentally or physically, if we simply allow ourselves to be in harmony. We don't have to adjust our vibration or become someone else; all we need to do is harmonize our energy with that of the people around us. All harmonizing takes is intending that you are in harmony. Close your eyes, picture the person or situation you want to create harmony with and intend it to be so. This process of setting your intention to create harmony removes the discordance between you and others and allows everyone's Truths to co-exist. Give harmonizing a try and see how your relationships shift and change.

Create

We are divinely blessed with the power to create the life we desire. We are hindered only by our own blocks and limitations. The key to creating what you desire is focusing not on outcomes, but on what you have great passion for. Creativity comes from passion and passion is an expression of our inner light. The more you place your attention on what you are passionate about, the more your higher-self will present opportunities that fulfill that passion. Creativity will spiral out and open you up to more and more. Allow yourself to expand, focus on what inspires great passion in you and watch your life move in magical ways. If you feel stuck, review where you are focusing your energy and redefine your passions. It is often our ego and mind, with their need to control, that stall our forward motion.

Celebrate

It's time to celebrate! Yes, you! Do it right now – whether you think you have something to celebrate or not. Celebrate the miracle of breathing; celebrate being alive; celebrate something you've accomplished or that you created. We are so focused on *doing* that we can skip the celebration that should come with creating and manifesting. Celebrating doesn't need to be extravagant. It can be as simple as doing a 'yay, me!' dance in your kitchen. Make a list of all the things you have accomplished, created, witnessed and experienced that deserve celebration and then dance your heart out. The more you celebrate what you have created, you confirm your desire to continue creating and expanding.

Health

Who takes care of you? Do you? If you do not take care of yourself, you will have nothing to give others when they need you. Look after yourself; make time for yourself. Making time for yourself is essential to living a balanced and healthy life. If you hear yourself saying, "I don't have time to take care of myself," it's a signal to evaluate your priorities. Reevaluate the state of your health and wellness. Take a look at your diet. Think about what you are choosing to eat. Before you take a bite or a sip, ask, "How does this serve me?" Consider going on a cleanse, investing in a massage, taking Pilates or yoga, or getting more sleep. Taking care of ourselves is a big step in living life consciously.

Consciousness

Consciousness pertains to how you walk through the world – with awareness or without it. When we live unconsciously, we have no concept of or don't care about how our actions affect others or the world. Think of the person who carelessly throws trash on the ground, with no concern for the environment or thought as to the aesthetic enjoyment of others who experience this place, now strewn with litter. When we live consciously, we take into consideration our impact on the world as well as the world's impact on us. Consciousness is a piece of our spiritual evolution. It is a state of being that is active, but requires nothing of us, other than our awareness. Where in your life can you live with greater consciousness? Look at the words you use; do they empower and encourage? Look at the information you hear and read; is it truthful or meant to manipulate and control you energetically? Look at the food you eat; does it support your health and wellness? There are so many aspects of existence where we can to step into conscious living. Look at everything in your life with these questions: Does this serve me? Does this support me? Does this empower me

See

Our sight is an active sense, but it can be easy to fall into a habit of seeing that causes us to miss a lot. What we see can become overshadowed by what we think we know, or by past experiences that obscure what is right in front of us. Think about what the ability to see means for a baby – everything he encounters is a new experience that holds great wonder and amazement. Take off the blinders of familiarity and start seeing your world with fresh eyes. Look at the colors around you and take in the nuances of shade, tone and hue. When you look at people, really see them for who they are in that moment. When you open up to seeing in present time and with conscious intention, what you see will not only inspire you; it will connect you more fully and deeply to the world that is yours.

Listen

When we listen, we form a response to what is being said. Be conscious of the way you filter and interpret the words you hear. Look for instances of responding or reacting based on past experience rather than to what is actually being said in the moment. Challenge yourself to listen consciously to people. Hear what it is that they are actually saying. Old filters can twist and color information and your response. When we are working to change something about ourselves, there is often a four step process involved: first we recognize our behavior afterward during reflection; then we begin to recognize our behavior while we are in the midst of a situation; from there we move to having an awareness of our behavior prior to stepping into it allowing us to choose another reaction; and finally we reach a point where the behavior no longer exists. Removing old filters and patterns will most likely follow this pattern. Take your time, be gentle with yourself and, most importantly, when you notice a reaction or a response that does not reflect conscious listening, envision a bubble out in front of you and intend that you are releasing the energy of that reaction or response. It's a simple, but powerful tool that will help you clean out everything that colors how you listen. This practice alone will change your life and tune you into the intent and meaning of other people's words.

Speaking

If you feel unheard at home or at work, reflect on how you are speaking. Are you speaking defensively? Are you speaking with accusation? Most of us have experienced some element of invalidation that has caused wounding. This invalidation can make what we have to say come out with an edge of some sort. People don't, won't or can't listen to our underlying message when we have that edge. If you aren't sure how you sound, record yourself in conversation throughout the day and then listen to how you present information. Listen for harshness and also for reservation or retreat. Remove the emotion and the preconceived notions from what you have to say and speak from a place of truth, certainty and knowingness. You'll be happily surprised by how much this shift will change your interactions with people.

Support

We tend to take on many responsibilities, both at work and at home, that stretch ourselves too thin. This tendency has an impact not only on our day-to-day life, but also on our health and wellness. Where does your support come from? Do you have enough? Could benefit from more? Whether your support comes from a group, family or friends, it's time to ask for help. Delegate responsibilities, let the little things slide and find time to nurture yourself and care for your own well-being.

Joy

Throughout our lives, expression of our joy is often stifled or altogether stopped. We become programmed to shorten or deaden it for fear that others won't be able to accept us as joyful. It is true that many people cannot accept being around joy, because it reminds them that they cannot and do not experience it themselves, but is that reason to stop yours from flowing? Possibly you have not even been aware of when and where you cut your own joy short. Joy flows up from inside of us from a place just below the base of the spine (just below the tailbone). To get your joy flowing, close your eyes and place your attention at the base of your spine. Imagine that you are turning on a faucet opening the stream of free-flowing joy. Imagine that the flow of joy is a color and by using your intention, move the energy of joy up your spine and allow it to fountain out the top of your head. Practice this short meditation daily to help you live life joyously.

Light

Are you hiding your light? Your light is the essence of you as a spiritual being, and it is in embracing your inner light that you live fully and completely. Anything less means you are limiting who you are and what you can have. So let it shine! That doesn't mean everyone will appreciate its brightness. What's important to know is that when people around you don't appreciate your brightness, you are not the problem; it's that your light shining causes them to see that theirs is not. This reaction in itself is one reason we hide ourselves, because those around us cannot accept us for all that we are. Subscribing to this way of thinking, plain and simple, keeps you living as less than who you truly are. Stop hiding your light and let it burn brightly.

Tools

There are many methods, or tools, for finding and maintaining balance in our daily lives. What tools do you have that help you manage day to day? What helps keep you balanced or sane? What reminds you to take a breath, to be in the moment or to experience life fully each and every day? Whether they're yoga, walking, singing, dancing, meditating, gardening, the tools throughout this book or other activities that balance you, see your tools for what they offer you, and then use them. If, after taking stock, you can truly say you have no tools, then it is time to find activities that will support your quest of living life consciously. Make time every day for tools that help you live a centered life.

Meditation

Meditation helps create a sense of grounding, balance and flow in your life. It connects your spirit and your body and allows you to live consciously and in present time. You might be familiar with the style of meditation that entails sitting cross-legged in contemplation. Practicing this style is about searching for enlightenment and transcending the body. Today, we are asked to recognize that we are already enlightened. Instead of working to transcend the body, we are asked to connect our spirit with our body, to access the true creative power that occurs when spirit and body are one.

Here is a simple, but powerful process that is about connecting: connecting our body to the earth and our spirit to our body. Sit in a chair with your feet flat on the floor, close your eyes and imagine that a beam of light connects from your tailbone down to the center of the earth. The only other thing to do is imagine that there is an on/off switch on the side of the chord and flip that switch on with your intention. This is your simple meditation. Sit in this space, connected to the earth. There is nothing to do, or that you need to try to achieve. Even if you've convinced yourself that you can't meditate, give it a try; you will be surprised. This truly simple process will help you feel more grounded, connected and centered and support you in living consciously.

Music

Music is energy. The way music vibrates within your body has an impact on your health, wellness and emotional and mental states. Incorporate music into your day and choose types that support your well-being and bring light into your day. Chants, whatever their derivation (Gregorian, Native American and Sanskrit are some examples), move and shift energy within you. Other forms, such as classical, affect the emotions and the mind.

Therapeutic music, which channels the voices and messages of the angels and goddess or uses tones that heal your chakras (energy centers of the body), lifts you up, while contemporary music engages you and gets your body moving. Experiment with different forms of music and make a point to remain conscious of what you're experiencing as you listen to each. Create a journal to record your findings. You will then be able to bring consciousness into your choice of music, have an awareness of the effect it has on you and use music to help you heal and grow.

Movement

Movement is essential for your life to flow. If your job entails sitting, be sure to get up and move throughout the day. Not only will this be good for your body, but it will also help move energy. If things have seemed "stuck" lately, get your body moving, and life movement will follow. Movement can also help you work through emotions and resolve problems that have your mind whirling. Whether you take a brisk walk, do yoga or Pilates or simply dance around the house, adding movement into your day will infuse your life with a greater sense of flow.

Adventure

The world is full of new beginnings and endless possibilities and our life is a grand adventure if we choose to see it in that way. Limitations on how we view life come from our beliefs. Approaching experiences as adventures, where there is always something to discover, whether that's about yourself or the world, will help break down these limiting beliefs. Take some time to think about your life as an adventure. Make a timeline and mark off all your life-changing experiences (good or bad); from the wonder of birth, to your first words or first steps, to learning how to drive and learning how to navigate relationships. Life can be viewed as one marvelous or bewildering or even sad experience after the other. Each experience is part of this grand adventure though offering lessons and healing – if we are conscious. Whatever the experience, our lives hold a never ending unfolding of next steps and new doors to open.

Nourish

Nourish yourself physically. As the energy on the planet moves faster and faster, our bodies are requiring cleaner fuel. Reflect on what you are putting into your body. Seek to remove foods from your diet that do not allow your body to vibrate at its highest vibration.

Nourish yourself energetically. It is equally important that way we nourish ourselves, by what we bring into our lives. Is what you watch, read, listen to and even the company you keep something that nourishes your mind, your heart, your soul and your vision for your life? Be sure to surround yourself with people and things that nourish who you want to be and how you want to live.

What are you doing to nourish yourself? If you are directing all of your energy and attention outside of yourself, giving to others, doing for others, supporting others, now is the time to focus on nourishing you. Take a bath, buy some flowers, make a beautiful meal or take a meditative walk – all of these are ways that you can nourish yourself

Embrace

Embrace your life rather than push it away. Embracing is a way of welcoming in and enfolding. If parts of your life are out of balance, find a way to embrace them, or love them, for what they offer you. The more you push them away, the greater your resistance becomes and, interestingly, the more energy you create around that piece or thing you are trying to push away. Everything in our life is there to teach or show us something about ourselves, the choices we make and the way in which we choose to live. Embrace what you have created, even if it isn't what you want, and once you've embraced it, set about changing it and creating what you do want.

Explore

Exploration invites us to peel away layers and search for deeper insight. Your exploration may be of a topic that interests you; dig deeper to access greater levels of awareness and information. Maybe your exploration is into your own approach to life; dig deeper to understand why you fear change or uncertainty or why you push away true love. Or maybe it is your own thoughts that you will explore; does what you think and believe come from your truth or the beliefs of others?

By encouraging yourself to explore your thoughts, your interests and the world around you will enhance your ability to live life consciously. As you search for deeper meaning in what you see, what you hear and what you know you will begin to develop an awareness of what resonates as true for you and what does not.

Encourage

Where other concepts have been a message to you, this one is a message for you. It is a message that encourages you to keep moving forward and striving to grow and step into the Truth that is your natural state of being. You are being encouraged to stand up for what you believe, to use your voice and to speak your Truth. You are being encouraged to surround yourself with beauty and vibrations that will inspire and uplift you. You are being encouraged to be you.

Expand

We are taught to contract and to pull ourselves in. But contracting creates limit, lack and stagnation in our lives and allows fear to take hold. When you are faced with challenges and obstacles, expand to move past them. Close your eyes and simply by intending it allow yourself to expand energetically --- to move out and beyond the constraints that keep you living in limitation. Also, think about how you might expand your life through the thoughts you have and the words you use. Pay attention to when you choose phrases like "I have to go to work." How much more expansive it is to say, "I have work to go to." Use your intention to expand yourself and consciously convert constricting thoughts, words, and experiences into expansion. Your life will flow with greater grace and ease as you do.

Patience

"In your patience you will possess your soul." -- St. Paul. So many people struggle with trying to "have patience." The point they are often missing is this: Like so many other things in our lives, lacking patience offers a key to our own healing and inner growth. To simply say "have patience" doesn't deal with the cause of impatience. A lack of patience is rooted in the invalidations and wounding we have experienced. Our impatience comes from feeling undervalued, unseen, unheard and pushed away. Finding patience requires understanding what triggers our impatience. Start a journal that allows you to reflect on the situations in which you experience impatience. Healing is simple. Once you can see the energies that contribute to your reactions, you can release those energies. You must release them, in fact, or you will continue to create opportunities that encourage you to release. It is your life's journey to be healed and to be whole.

Calm

Have you seen a duck treading water? It looks calm on the surface, but below in the water its feet are paddling like crazy. Just like that duck's feet, there's a voice within you that has you going around and around and around. Quieting that voice will help you find inner calm. Whether that voice is critical, fearful, angry or restrictive, you have the choice to listen to and feed into it or not. This voice tends to create worry, frenzy, fear or anger, all of which are toxic energies to the body, because they create an acidic environment in which disease can take hold. Use your breath and blow these energies free from your body. Look for the thoughts that create anything but calm and set your sights on erasing these. Quiet the mind with deep breathing so you can find and create calm within.

Breathe

When you breathe, you are both cleansing the body and connecting the body to your spirit. Our breath is one of the most powerful and easily accessible healing tools that we possess. Deep breathing helps release stagnant emotional energy, while physically it slows the heart rate and creates a sense of calm and well-being. When we are fearful, angry, in physical pain or under attack, we tend to hold our breath. At those times, if you can focus on deep breathing, you will find that you move through the situations with greater ease. Become aware of your breath as it moves through your body. Your breath will seek out and help you identify the areas where you hold tension in your body. If you find tension or pain, you can release it with your breath, by envisioning that you are breathing into the area affected. Directing your breath in this way will help clear the energy that has the tension or pain locked in place.

Stepping Into a Conscious Life - The Choice of a Lifetime

Conscious Living is *The Choice of a Lifetime.*

When we choose to live life consciously we wake-up to all the amazing aspects of being alive; from the journey that we are on to the work that we are doing to evolve our own Spirit and that of the collective.

When we live consciously we begin to see that all things are interconnected and there is both magic and power in this awareness.

When we live consciously we are truly living. The blinders come off and a whole new way of seeing the world and living in the world spring to life

When we live consciously we wake-up to all the many ways in which our lives are put together and our destiny becomes ours to consciously create. Some people spend their entire life living unconsciously, unaware of why their life unfolds the way it does and allowing their unconsciousness to drag them along. Life is only 'by chance' if we are unconscious to it. There is so much richness and reward that comes when we live with awareness.

As you take this step toward conscious living, from this day on, each step you take must be made as a conscious choice.

We are no longer able to sit and wait for something greater than ourselves – God, The Universe, The One - to tell us what to do. Our learning, our healing, our growth will only happen when we say 'yes' to the steps along the way.

Feeling Stuck?

As you move forward with Conscious Living, if you find yourself feeling stuck consider several things:

Are you out of alignment? If you step out of alignment, life can feel like it screeches to a halt. If you notice that things don't seem to be moving smoothly, that things that used to bother you are back – revisit the alignment exercise from part one and get yourself back on-track.

Is your mind trying to run the show? When our mind gets activated we lose our connection to Spirit and naturally fall out of alignment. Return to the exercise to Quiet Your Mind in part one.

Is your ego ruling the day? The ego can pull us out of conscious living by its need to be seen and its need to control the flow of life by pushing rather than by allowing. If you've stepped into ego, revisit the importance of self-validation and then realign with Spirit.

Choose 'YES". Choose to take your next step. If you are in alignment, the mind is quiet and the ego has surrendered to the knowingness of Spirit – choose 'yes'. As we move down the road of Conscious Living we can reach stages where we must say 'Yes, I want to move forward. Yes, I want to continue on this conscious journey' These moments act as gate keepers, pushing you to be aware of your actions and pushing you to consciously choose the path of your own unfolding and ever evolving life.

When we live consciously we come to see that life is only predestined when we sleep our way through it. When we wake up and begin to understand the purpose of our lives and the power that we hold, life is what we choose. Life is the choice of our lifetime.

Say 'Yes'! to everything that leads you down your path to consciousness. Conscious Living asks us to be aware in all aspects of our life – money, health and wellness, education, culturally, socially, parenting, relationships…it's time to wake-up in each and every area of your life.

What we eat, drink, see, listen to; the way we speak, interact and respond; we can bring conscious awareness to each and every aspect of our life and in doing so, we create a *whole-being* experience where we are fully activated as a conscious, living, spirit.

TOOL TO HELP YOU BRING CONSCIOUS AWARENESS TO ALL AREAS OF YOUR LIFE

To help you assess the various areas of your life
- Use your journal or the Conscious Living Playbook (which has a place to explore this exercise) and list each of these seven areas as a header on separate pages: Relationships, Finance, Hearth and Home, Health and Wellness, Environment, Family, and Nutrition
- For each of these areas explore:
    - The way in which they show up in your life?
    - What is your experience with them?
    - Have you been floating along?
    - Can you identify unconsciousness?

- If yes, what does unconsciousness look like for example – what does unconsciousness look like in your money space or financially?
- Feel free to look at both your personal experience as well as on a more global level if that interests you. We can learn so much by looking at the whole. I see us as microcosms of the macrocosm – so what we are working on, the planet is working on and vice versa.
- Next for each area, apply the concepts and tools in this book to the energy dynamics of these areas. As everything is energy, it is not only our personal growth that we can support, but we can energetically support the areas of our life and help to guide these into consciousness as well.
  - For example – let's use the money space again – you can employ the concepts of expand, creating greater room for money to come in. Or Harmony as a way of setting your money space in attunement with your inner and outer world. Or even alignment, placing your manifestation of money in alignment with your Spirit.

Once you have awareness and tools to play with, there is no limit to the way in which you can play!

Lastly remember that stepping into awareness is a process, you may have great days and not-so great days. Some days you will be so in alignment and connected the experience will be exhilarating and inspiring. Other days you will step out of consciousness, out of alignment and find yourself struggling. Days like these are the reminders as to why living consciously matters. Days like these show you what happens when you don't live with awareness.

These days show you how your life used to be, before you had awareness, before you had the experience of Conscious Living.

Also it's important to remember that our healing happens in layers. As we unpeel the layers of our unconsciousness, it may seem like we keep working on the same thing, or you may find yourself saying "but I already did this!" We have layers and layers of information, programming and energy to clear away.

But it is in this process, that we prepare for the power that comes when we live consciously. I mentioned this at the beginning of the book. Ultimate Conscious Living is a state of being in which we are fully connected and fully empowered. We don't get to have ultimate Conscious Living until we can demonstrate that we can handle it.

The unpeeling of layers gives us countless opportunities to prepare and to say 'yes' to our own growth. We can always say 'I've had enough, this is far enough or let me take a little break' but as it is part of our Spiritual evolution, your own Spirit will continue to prod you to move forward.

Remember, life is a journey and spiritual evolution is a spiral. Living a conscious life puts you in the driver's seat of your own magnificently spiraling journey

.

ABOUT THE AUTHOR

Christine Agro is an inspiring metaphysical expert. As a clairvoyant, empowering teacher and natural healer, she has been helping people understand and embrace the true beauty of being here on this planet.

She has been sharing her unique approach to health, wellness and conscious living for more than 12 years. Christine provides a truly holistic overview, whether in one-on-one sessions, in courses and workshops or speaking. Praised by grateful women, parents, animal guardians and celebrity clients across the globe for her intuitive and extraordinary gifts as a healer, she has been hailed as "magical", "transformational" and "inspiring."

Christine has been featured in The New York Times and has been interviewed on radio shows around the world, quoted in health and consumer magazines and e-zines nationwide and is the founder of The Conscious Living Guide ™.

In 2001 Christine graduated from the School of Natural Medicine with degrees in Naturopathy, Western Herbs, Iridology, and Natural Physician. She also completed three years of Clairvoyant study at the Inner Connection Institute in Denver Colorado. In 2000 Christine received her Raw Foods Teacher Certification from the Ann Wigmore Institute in Puerto Rico and Christine received her Yoga Teacher Certification from the Shambavanda School of Yoga based in Colorado.

Christine lives outside of NYC and shares her life with her husband Chuck and son Caidin as well as Brew the dog, Cassie the Cat, Cha Cha Blue the Parakeet and all the animals who visit her daily.

CONSCIOUS LIVING WISDOM CARDS

Conscious Living Wisdom Cards include the 42 Conscious Living Concepts with a booklet that explains all 42 concepts. Use this deck to remind you to live life consciously and to help give you guidance and insight throughout the day or whenever you need it. This deck is the size of a regular deck of cards and fits easily in your purse, backpack or brief case. Take it with you, leave it on your desk, share it with friends!

Order yours today at TheConsciousLivingGuide.com or register as 3 month or 12 month Basic member at TCLG and get the deck for free. (While supplies last)

WORK WITH CHRISTINE AGRO

Private Sessions
Christine Agro offers private session to help you explore your own life's journey. During a reading she can explore anything that's going on in your life. The only thing Christine doesn't do is future tell.

Christine uses her unique ability to see all things as energy to give you guidance, insight and clarity into your relationships, health and wellness, parent/child relationships and animal relationships. All readings are done by phone. Email Christine at Christine@christineagro.com to set-up and appointment

Classes and Workshops
Christine offers numerous course, classes and workshops where she teaches you how to tap into your own inner guidance. All of Christine's programs are experiential. During every class Christine introduces tools that can help you live consciously and she guides you through using these tools, right in class. Classes and workshops are held on-line, via webinar and in person on request.

Tools to Live By – a six week program that introduces six powerful tools. When these tools are combined they form a simple but powerful meditation process that can help you create the life you desire. Learn to ground, hold your space, release energy that doesn't belong to you and find a place of neutrality. Class meets via teleconference or become a member of The Conscious Living Guide and add-on Tools to Live By as a pre-recorded program.

12 Month Clairvoyant and Conscious Living Program – This life changing program helps students tap into their own clairvoyance and learn numerous ways to self-heal. Students also learn how to read clairvoyantly, the important of which rests in the ability to gain your own information and insight. We meet twice a week for a total of 48 weeks. Class is held via teleconference so students can attend from anywhere in the world.

Visit AwakenandGrow.com for updated course schedules.

NOTES

NOTES

Thank you for being here!

www.ingramcontent.com/pod-product-compliance
Lightning Source LLC
Chambersburg PA
CBHW051453290426
44109CB00016B/1742